Praying the Word

From the Book of Galatians

By

L. O. Ovbije

ISBN: 978-1-944411-03-9

Copyright © 2018 by Rev. L O. Ovbije

Ovbije World Outreach Ministries, Inc.

Published by SOIL Foundation, Inc.

P.O. Box 966

Clarkston, GA 30021-0966

U. S. A.

Website: owom.org

Email: theword@owom.org

Published by SOIL Foundation, Inc.

P.O. Box 966

Clarkston, GA 30021-0966

U. S. A.

All scriptures are from King James Version (KJV)

Printed in the United States of America.

DEDICATION

To God the Father, who love the world he created and sent Jesus Christ his only begotten Son into the world, To Jesus Christ who came into this world in the flesh, died, buried and rose from the dead triumphantly to redeem every human being God created and God made in his own image and likeness, this Jesus Christ of Nazareth has made redemption available for any human being that will trust and believe in him. And to the Holy Spirit, who continuously reveal Jesus Christ to individuals and people daily.

I thank God for my dear father who taught me discipline and my precious mother who taught me grace and forgiveness. Both taught me unconditional love. Both love me unconditionally.

Pray in the language you speak daily. Do not pray to impress people or God. There is no language on earth that is superior to your language. Pray in your own language. Pray in the language you understand, God wants to hear from you now.

I Timothy 3:16

ACKNOWLEDGMENTS

To my wonderful parents, Chief J. E. Ovbije & Mrs. Margaret O. Ovbije, and to my siblings. My father was a man that lived a life that left an excellent and lasting impression on me. My father and mother taught me unconditional love; my mother taught me grace and forgiveness. Our family knew the meaning of a loving, secure and rich home because of my father's presence. I thank God for the private elementary school at Sapele: Children Nursery School, where I attended. It was there that I encounter God for the first time in prayer in a very early age.

To my precious pastor and his lovely wife, both were strong examples of a man and a woman devoted to God. I was fortunate to have pastor & Mrs. Umukoro, both disciple me. I thank them both for their daily early Morning Prayer life. To the men of God who also impacted my prayer life, W. F. Kumuyi and Benjamin Udi.

Finally to my sweet, precious, wonderful wife Theresa Spearman Ovbije, a woman of God, whom I simply call "sweetie".

CHAPTER ONE

¹ Paul, an apostle, (not of men, neither by man, but by Jesus Christ, and God the Father, who raised him from the dead;)

Father in the name of Jesus, I thank you that you called me through Jesus Christ. Father I thank you that no one else called me but you alone called me and anointed me. Father I thank you that my calling is not by any religious groups, or by good works but by your grace through Jesus Christ, in Jesus name, Amen.

² And all the brethren which are with me, unto the churches of Galatia:

Father in the name of Jesus, I thank you that your word is for my edification, admonishment, training, correction and to build me up. Father I thank you that I am part of the Church which is the body of Christ, in Jesus name, Amen.

³ Grace be to you and peace from God the Father, and from our Lord Jesus Christ,

Father in Jesus name, I thank you that I do receive your grace and peace daily through Jesus Christ my Lord, in Jesus name, Amen.

⁴ Who gave himself for our sins, that he might deliver us from this present evil world, according to the will of God and our Father:

Father in the name of Jesus, I thank you for the vicarious sacrifice of Jesus Christ, I thank you for Jesus Christ, who gave his life for me, I thank you for the precious blood of Jesus Christ shed for the remission of my sins, Father I thank you for Jesus Christ who delivered me from this evil world according to your will, therefore, with my own mouth I boldly declare my deliverance now and forever, in Jesus name, Amen.

[5] To whom be glory for ever and ever. Amen.

Father in Jesus name, to you and you alone I give all the glory, honour and thanksgiving for the sacrifice of Jesus Christ for me and my deliverance, in Jesus name, Amen.

[6] I marvel that ye are so soon removed from him that

called you into the grace of Christ unto another gospel:

Father in Jesus name, I pray that I will not remove myself from the grace of Christ. Father I pray that whatever I hear, I will always judge it by your word, no matter who said it. Father I thank you that I do esteem your word above everything. Father I thank you that I am establish in the grace of my Lord and Saviour Jesus Christ. Father I thank you that you made Jesus Christ righteousness for me and to me. Jesus Christ is my righteousness and I am God's righteousness in Christ Jesus, in Jesus name, Amen.

[7] Which is not another; but there be some that trouble you, and would pervert the gospel of Christ.

Father in Jesus name, I thank you that I am establish in Jesus Christ and his righteousness. I refuse to go back to good works and religion. Father I thank you that if it is works then it is no more grace, and if it is grace then it is no more works, so, Father I thank you that since I did not save myself, but I am saved by grace through faith in Christ Jesus, therefore I stand by grace and I live by the faith of my Lord and Saviour Jesus Christ who loved me and gave himself for me, in Jesus name, Amen.

[8] But though we, or an angel from heaven, preach any other gospel unto you than that which we have preached unto you, let him be accursed.

Father in Jesus name, I thank you for your written word, Father through your grace I am committed to judge every preaching, every messages and revelation by your written word, regardless who it is coming from, for everything is subject to your written word, in Jesus name, Amen.

⁹ As we said before, so say I now again, if any man preach any other gospel unto you than that ye have received, let him be accursed.

Father I will not preach nor receive any gospel that denied Jesus Christ death, buried, and resurrection. I will not preach or receive any gospel that deny Jesus Christ is the Way, the Truth and the Life, I will not preach or receive any gospel that deny Jesus Christ is the only Way to God and to salvation, in Jesus name, Amen.

¹⁰ For do I now persuade men, or God? or do I seek to please men? for if I yet pleased men, I should not be the servant of Christ.

Father in Jesus name, I thank you for the grace not to please man or anyone but to only please him who loved me gave himself for me, Yes, Jesus only, to please him alone with my spirit, soul and body. To live my life for him, Jesus Christ who bluntly refused to compromise, in Jesus name, Amen.

¹¹ But I certify you, brethren, that the gospel which was preached of me is not after man.

Father in the name of Jesus, I thank you that this Jesus Christ whom I be-lieve with all my heart: is more than a mere man, more than a theologian, more than a good teacher, more than a good moral person, more than a person of history, he is your only begotten Son. He is the only Redeemer for the whole world, in Jesus name, Amen.

[12] For I neither received it of man, neither was I taught it, but by the revelation of Jesus Christ.

Father in the name of Jesus, I thank you that flesh and blood cannot inherit your Kingdom, Father I thank you, for that which is born of the flesh is flesh, and that which is born of the Spirit is spirit, for no person can come to Jesus Christ except you draw them by your Spirit. Father I thank you that I do preach, teach, and share the gospel of Jesus Christ by revelation, not by what I heard other preachers preach or teach, but by your Word, by your revelation that does not contradict your Word, and by my intimate relation with you, in Jesus name, Amen.

¹³ For ye have heard of my conversation in time past in the Jews' religion, how that beyond measure I persecuted the church of God, and wasted it:

Father in Jesus name, I thank you for salvation, before I accepted Jesus Christ into my heart, going to Church was a ritual and Christianity was to me just been a good person and be nice, but I am forever grateful to you for your grace which brought the revelation of Jesus Christ to me in my spiritual ignorant state of mind, Father I thank you, in Jesus name, Amen.

¹⁴ And profited in the Jews' religion above many my

equals in mine own nation, being more exceedingly zealous of the traditions of my fathers.

Father in the name of Jesus, I thank you that tradition of men was Ok, before the glorious light of the gospel of my Lord Jesus Christ shine into my heart. Those works and traditions that made me feel good are but vain to me now that Christ is in me the hope of glory, in Jesus name, Amen.

¹⁵ But when it pleased God, who separated me from my mother's womb, and called me by his grace,

Father in Jesus name, I thank you that you called me while I was in my mother's womb. Father I thank you that society did not called me, the religious organization did not called me,

Father you called me, anointed me and ordain me for your glory and to bring forth fruit for your glory. Father I thank you that I am not ashamed of the gospel of Christ Jesus, which I preach, for it is your power unto salvation to everyone that believe, in Jesus name, Amen.

¹⁶ To reveal his Son in me, that I might preach him among the heathen; immediately I conferred not with flesh and blood:

Father in Jesus name, I thank you that I have accepted Jesus Christ, Father I thank you that Christ is in me, and Christ in me is the hope of glory, I thank you that you do reveal Jesus Christ in me and through me daily. I thank you that my relationship with you is not religion, and I am not involved in religious rituals, in Jesus name, Amen.

¹⁷ Neither went I up to Jerusalem to them which were apostles before me; but I went into Arabia, and returned again unto Damascus.

Father in Jesus name, I thank you that my relationship with you is not based on any preacher, or any Church committee, is not based on any Church membership or members, is not based on any religious rituals, but it is based on the person of my Lord and Saviour Jesus Christ and his shed precious blood. Therefore, Father I thank you that nobody can separate me from your love which is in Christ Jesus my Lord, in Jesus name, Amen.

¹⁸ Then after three years I went up to Jerusalem to see

Peter, and abode with him fifteen days.

Father in Jesus name, I thank you that I do fellowship with other believers in Christ. Father I thank you for the sweet fellowship I do have with you daily, and I thank you for the fellowship I do have with other believers, in Jesus name, Amen.

¹⁹ But other of the apostles saw I none, save James the Lord's brother.

Father in Jesus name, I thank you that your word said we should pray one for another and to remember the brethren that are suffering, Father I pray that you will strengthen the inner man of the saints that are suffering for the sake of the gospel of Jesus Christ in various countries, I pray that they will not forsake Jesus Christ, in Jesus name, Amen.

²⁰ Now the things which I write unto you, behold, before God, I lie not.

Father in Jesus name, I thank you that your word said we should not lie one to another, Father I thank you that your word said we should speak the truth in love. Father I thank you that the Spirit of Truth does dwell in me, therefore, I have no desire to lie and I do speak the truth in love, for I do stand by your grace, in Jesus name, Amen.

²¹ Afterwards I came into the regions of Syria and Cilicia;

Father I thank you that I am a written epistle of Christ ready by all. Father I thank you that I am not ashamed of the gospel of Christ, for it is your power unto salvation. Therefore, I do look for opportunity or create an opportunity to share the gospel, in Jesus name, Amen.

²² And was unknown by face unto the churches of Judaea which were in Christ:

Father in Jesus name, I thank you that I do accept fellow Christians as Christ accepted me. Father I pray that fellow Christians will accept one another as Jesus Christ accepted us, I pray that I or any Christians will not judge another Christian on the base of denomination, religious belief and the tradition of men that make the word of God of none effect, in Jesus name, Amen.

²³ But they had heard only, That he which persecuted us in times past now preacheth the faith which once he destroyed.

Father in Jesus name, I pray that I will not judge any believer in Christ base on their past life and life style. I pray that I will see fellow believers in Christ as you see them, that I will see each believer as a new creature in Christ. Father I pray that I will always reminded myself that individual Christians are growing in grace, and that instead of judging them, that I will intercede for them till Christ be formed in them, in Jesus name, Amen.

²⁴ And they glorified God in me.

Father in the name of Jesus Christ of Nazareth, I pray that wherever I go and wherever I am, that people will see Jesus Christ in me and through me, and that you will be glorify in me. Father I thank you that my life does magnify you and the risen Christ, my life does emit the sweet fragrance of Christ, in Jesus name, Amen.

CHAPTER TWO

¹ Then fourteen years after I went up again to Jerusalem with Barnabas, and took Titus with me also.

Father in the name of Jesus, I thank you that you sent your followers out in pair, Father I thank you that where two or three are gathered together in the name of Jesus, you are there in the midst of them, in Jesus name, Amen.

² And I went up by revelation, and communicated unto them that gospel which I preach among the Gentiles, but privately to them which were of reputation, lest by

any means I should run, or had run, in vain.

Father in Jesus name, I thank you that a revelation given to the masses is not of private interpretation. Father I thank you that you are not the author of confusion. Father I thank you that your word said that no prophecy of the scripture is of any private interpretation, in Jesus name, Amen.

³ But neither Titus, who was with me, being a Greek, was compelled to be circumcised:

Father in Jesus name, I thank you that circumcision or uncircumcision availed anything but a new creature. It is faith in the finished work of Jesus Christ that account for righteousness. Father I pray that I will always glory in you and not glory in good works, in Jesus name, Amen.

4 **And that because of false brethren unawares brought in, who came in privily to spy out our liberty which we have in Christ Jesus, that they might bring us into bondage:**

Father in the name of Jesus Christ, I thank you for the liberty Christ Jesus gave to me in salvation. Father I am very aware that there are some religious folks who are very jealous of the joy those of us who are born again are enjoying in you. Father I thank you for the joy of my salvation. Who the Son set free, is free indeed. Jesus has set me free; I refuse to be put in bondage, in Jesus name, Amen.

5 **To whom we gave place by subjection, no, not for an hour; that the truth of the**

gospel might continue with you.

Father in the name of Jesus, I thank you that by your grace I am standing firmly daily in Christ and refusing to entangle with any yoke of bondage, in Jesus name, Amen.

⁶ But of these who seemed to be somewhat, (whatsoever they were, it maketh no matter to me: God accepteth no man's person:) for they who seemed to be somewhat in conference added nothing to me:

Father I thank you in Jesus name, that you are no respecter of person. Father I thank you that you are not partial like some religious people or non-religious people are, neither do you look at the outward appearance of people. But, Father you search the heart of individuals and you know the motives of individuals. Individuals may deceive others but none can deceive you. So, Father I thank you that it is not what people thinks of me that matters, it is what you think and say about me that matter. Father in Jesus name by your grace I am committed to obey you rather than people, in Jesus name, Amen.

[7] But contrariwise, when they saw that the gospel of the uncircumcision was committed unto me, as the gospel of the circumcision was unto Peter;

Father in the name of Jesus Christ, I thank you for committing to me the gospel of grace. Father I am committed to live, preach and share this gospel of the grace of my Lord Jesus Christ with others, in Jesus name, Amen.

⁸ (For he that wrought effectually in Peter to the apostleship of the circumcision, the same was mighty in me toward the Gentiles:)

Father in Jesus name, I thank you for your Holy Spirit that came into me in salvation, I thank you for the baptism of the Holy Ghost with fire, Father I thank you that you that anointed Apostle Peter, Apostle Paul and all that are born again, has also anointed me because I am born again. Father I thank you that you have anointed all the women that are born again. Father in the name of Jesus, your word said whatsoever I bound on earth is bound in heaven, so Father in Jesus name I bound every demonic spirit that will use religion to oppress any woman that is born again. Father I pray that every born again woman in the world will rise up and obey your anointing that is in each of them which you have given to each them. in Jesus name, Amen.

⁹ And when James, Cephas, and John, who seemed to be pillars, perceived the grace that was given unto me, they gave to me and Barnabas the right hands of fellowship; that we should go unto the heathen, and they unto the circumcision.

Father in the name of Jesus Christ, I thank you that those around me know that I am anointed; they do see the manifestation of Jesus Christ in me. I am not ashamed to say boldly that I am anointed, yes; I am anointed by God Almighty. He that is in me is greater than he that is in the world, in Jesus name, Amen.

¹⁰ Only they would that we should remember the poor; the same which I also was forward to do.

Father in the name of Jesus, I thank you that you said that he that hath pity upon the poor lend unto the LORD; and that which he hath given will you pay him again. Father I thank you that by your grace I will continue to reach out to the poor with substance, yes I will share your blessing in my life with the poor. In the name of Jesus, I will give to the poor spiritual things and material things, in Jesus name, Amen.

¹¹ But when Peter was come to Antioch, I withstood him to the face, because he was to be blamed.

Father in the name of Jesus, I thank you for the grace not to endorse any

wrong done by anyone in any leadership position. I pray that I will always
speak the truth in love. Father I thank
you that you have not given me the
spirit of timidity but you have given
me the spirit of power, and of love,
and of a sound mind. Father I pray that
I will always put your word above me
and anybody regardless who he or she
may be, I boldly declare I am no respecter of persons, in Jesus name,
Amen.

**12 For before that certain
came from James, he did eat
with the Gentiles: but when
they were come, he withdrew
and separated himself, fear-
ing them which were of the
circumcision.**

Father in the name of Jesus, I pray by
your grace that I will not compromise
your word because of religious people,

I pray that I will always be true to your word regardless where I am and who is around me. Father, I pray that I will always please you rather than people, in Jesus name, Amen.

^{13} And the other Jews dissembled likewise with him; insomuch that Barnabas also was carried away with their dissimulation.

Father in Jesus name, I thank you for sanctifying me by thou truth, thou word is truth, Father I thank you that I will not put any preacher, pastor, or bishop above your word, I pray that I will forever be a student of your word. I pray that I will always hungry for your word. Father I pray that I will always stay in your word, in Jesus name, Amen.

¹⁴ But when I saw that they walked not uprightly according to the truth of the gospel, I said unto Peter before them all, If thou, being a Jew, livest after the manner of Gentiles, and not as do the Jews, why compellest thou the Gentiles to live as do the Jews?

Father in the name of Jesus, I pray that I will not put any preacher above your word. I pray that I will never justify any preacher lifestyle that is contrary to your word. Father keeps me as the apple of your eyes. Father I pray that I will always look to Jesus, who is the author and finisher of my faith, in Jesus name, Amen.

¹⁵ We who are Jews by nature, and not sinners of the Gentiles,

Father in the name of Jesus, I thank you that it is not where we were born and what earthly family we were born into that matter, but being born again by your word that is what matter. Father I thank you that except an individual is born again, that individual cannot see you, Father I thank you that religion cannot birth the new birth, good works cannot birth the new birth, good moral and morality cannot birth the new birth, but it is your Holy Spirit alone that birth the new birth, when an individual put his or her faith in Jesus Christ and the finished work of Jesus Christ. I do deliberately and boldly put my faith in Jesus Christ and his finished work. I accept Jesus Christ into my heart now, in Jesus name, Amen.

¹⁶ Knowing that a man is not justified by the works of the law, but by the faith of Jesus Christ, even we have believed in Jesus Christ, that we might be justified by the faith of Christ, and not by the works of the law: for by the works of the law shall no flesh be justified.

Father in the name of Jesus, I thank you that I am not justified by my keeping of the law or by my good works, but I am justified by my faith in the finished work of Jesus Christ. It is not what I did or what I can do, but what Jesus Christ did, that gave me justification. Father I thank you that you gave me the faith to trust and believe the finished work of Jesus Christ, in Jesus name, Amen.

¹⁷ But if, while we seek to be justified by Christ, we ourselves also are found sinners, is therefore Christ the minister of sin? God forbid.

Father in Jesus name, I thank you that Jesus Christ is not and will never be minister of sin. Father I thank you that by your grace I will not allow religious folks to intimidate me about my liberty in Christ Jesus, I refuse in Jesus name to live in religious rituals. I do live in Christ and in God's law of love, in Jesus name, Amen.

¹⁸ For if I build again the things which I destroyed, I make myself a transgressor.

Father in Jesus name, I thank you that now that I am born again and I am a new creature in Christ Jesus, I do not go back to my old way of thinking, nor doing things that are not pleasing to you, in Jesus name. Amen.

[19] For I through the law am dead to the law, that I might live unto God.

Father in Jesus name, I am dead to the law, yes, I am free from the law, and I do now live forever unto God and Christ who loved me and gave himself for me, in Jesus name, Amen.

[20] I am crucified with Christ: nevertheless I live; yet not I, but Christ liveth in me: and the life which I now live in the flesh I live by the faith of the Son of God, who loved me, and gave himself for me.

Father in the name of Jesus, I thank you that the moment I accepted Jesus

Christ into my heart as my Saviour and Lord, I boldly identify with his crucifixion, buried, and resurrection. And, now that I am born again, I do live by the faith of Jesus Christ the Son of God who loved me and gave himself for me, in Jesus name, Amen.

21 I do not frustrate the grace of God: for if righteousness come by the law, then Christ is dead in vain.

Father in the name of Jesus Christ, I thank you that I did not received my righteousness which is of Christ by good deeds nor by keeping some of the laws or religious rituals, but I received your righteousness which is of Christ by faith in the finished work of Jesus Christ. Father I thank you that Christ did not died in vain. Father I thank you that Christ does live in me, in Jesus name, Amen.

CHAPTER THREE

¹ O foolish Galatians, who hath bewitched you, that ye should not obey the truth, before whose eyes Jesus Christ hath been evidently set forth, crucified among you?

Father in the name of Jesus, I thank you that I do have the mind of Christ, Father I thank you that I am your obedient child, Father I thank you that I do not follow religion but I am following Christ daily, in Jesus name, Amen.

² This only would I learn of you, Received ye the Spirit by the works of the law, or by the hearing of faith?

Father in the name of Jesus, I thank you that I did not receive your Spirit by keeping the law or by my good works. I did receive your Spirit by the hearing of faith in Jesus Christ and in his finished works, in Jesus name, Amen.

[3] Are ye so foolish? having begun in the Spirit, are ye now made perfect by the flesh?

Father in the name of Jesus, I thank you that I do walk in the spirit and not in the flesh, Father I thank you that your word said that I am in the spirit and not in the flesh, I boldly proclaim I am in the spirit and I am not in the flesh, in Christ I live, move and have my being, in Jesus name, Amen.

⁴ Have ye suffered so many things in vain? if it be yet in vain.

Father in the name of Jesus, I thank you that my suffering for Christ's sake and the gospel is not in vain. Father I thank you that I do reckon that the suffering of this present time is not worthy to be compare with the glory which shall be reveal in me, in Jesus name, Amen.

⁵ He therefore that ministereth to you the Spirit, and worketh miracles among you, doeth he it by the works of the law, or by the hearing of faith?

Father in the name of Jesus, I thank you that signs and wonder does follow me because I am a believer in Jesus

Christ, not because of my good works or because I am a Church member, or because of my gender, but simply because I am a believer in Jesus Christ, Father I thank you that your word said if a believer in Jesus Christ lay his or her hands on the sick in the name of Jesus, the sick shall recover, your word said that the believer shall cast out devil in the name of Jesus, Father I thank you that these are some signs that do follow the believer in Christ, Father I thank you that I am a believer and the signs Jesus Christ said in St. Mark 16:17-18 does follow me, in Jesus name, Amen.

[6] Even as Abraham believed God, and it was accounted to him for righteousness.

Father in the name of Jesus, I thank you that the moment I accepted Jesus Christ into my heart as my Lord and Saviour, you declared me righteous and you made Jesus Christ unto me righteousness. Father I thank you that I am your righteousness in Christ Jesus, in Jesus name, Amen.

⁷ Know ye therefore that they which are of faith, the same are the children of Abraham.

Father in the name of Jesus, I thank you that I am of faith and I am the child of faithful Abraham by promise, in Jesus name, Amen.

⁸ And the scripture, foreseeing that God would justify the heathen through faith, preached before the gospel unto Abraham, saying, In thee shall all nations be blessed.

Father in the name of Jesus, I thank you that I am justify, just as if I have never sin, Father I thank you that the very moment I placed my faith and trust in Jesus Christ and his finished works, you justified me and declared me righteous, in Jesus name, Amen.

[9] So then they which be of faith are blessed with faithful Abraham.

Father in the name of Jesus, I thank you that I am of faith and I am blessed with faithful Abraham. Father I thank you that Abraham believed you and you imputed righteousness to him, Father I believed in your only begotten Son Jesus Christ and his finished works, you declared me righteous and you made Christ Jesus unto me wisdom, and righteousness, and sanctification, and redemption. Father I do glory in you, in Jesus name, Amen.

¹⁰ For as many as are of the works of the law are under the curse: for it is written, Cursed is every one that continueth not in all things which are written in the book of the law to do them.

Father in the name of Jesus, I thank you that Jesus Christ has redeemed me from the curse of the law been made curse for me. Father I thank you that I am no longer under the law because I have accepted Jesus Christ into my heart as my Saviour and Lord, in Jesus name, Amen.

¹¹ But that no man is justified by the law in the sight of God, it is evident: for, The just shall live by faith.

Father in the name of Jesus, I thank you that I am not Justified by the law because the law did not saved me but I am justified by faith in Jesus Christ who loved me and gave himself for me. And, I do live by the faith of Jesus Christ, who justified me. Father I thank you that I do live by faith, for whatever is not of faith is sin, Father I thank you that I do not live in sin, but I do live by faith, in Jesus name, Amen.

12 And the law is not of faith: but, The man that doeth them shall live in them.

Father in the name of Jesus, I thank you that I do not live by the law, Father I thank you that I do live by faith, for the just shall live by faith, in Jesus name, Amen.

13 Christ hath redeemed us from the curse of the law, be-

ing made a curse for us: for it is written, Cursed is every one that hangeth on a tree:

Father in the name of Jesus Christ, I thank you that Jesus Christ has redeemed me from the curse of the law being made curse for me, for as it is written curse is every one that is hang on a tree. Father I thank you that Jesus Christ death publicly demonstrated your love for me publicly, in Jesus name, Amen.

[14] That the blessing of Abraham might come on the Gentiles through Jesus Christ; that we might receive the promise of the Spirit through faith.

Father in Jesus name, I thank you for the blessing of Abraham that has come to me through Jesus Christ, Father I do receive the blessing of Abraham you have given to me through Jesus Christ my Lord, in Jesus name, Amen.

¹⁵ Brethren, I speak after the manner of men; Though it be but a man's covenant, yet if it be confirmed, no man disannulleth, or addeth thereto.

Father in the name of Jesus Christ, I thank you that your covenant with me is an everlasting covenant sealed in the precious blood of Jesus Christ and it cannot be disannulled, Father in Jesus name I judge you faithful who has promised, in Jesus name, Amen.

¹⁶ Now to Abraham and his seed were the promises made. He saith not, And to seeds, as of many; but as of

one, And to thy seed, which is Christ.

Father in Jesus name, I thank you that Jesus Christ is the Way, the Truth and the Life. Father I thank you that Jesus Christ is the only person that paid the ultimate and vicarious price for the sins of the whole world. Father I thank you that Jesus Christ is the only Way to you, every other way or ways leads to religion, in Jesus name, Amen.

[17] And this I say, that the covenant, that was confirmed before of God in Christ, the law, which was four hundred and thirty years after, cannot disannul, that it should make the promise of none effect.

Father in the name of Jesus, I thank you for the covenant that you made in the blood of Jesus Christ with me, I thank you that this blood covenant is sure and Jesus Christ is the Surety. I thank you Father that this blood covenant is better and it is on a better promise. This covenant cannot be disannulled, in Jesus name, Amen.

[18] For if the inheritance be of the law, it is no more of promise: but God gave it to Abraham by promise.

Father in the name of Jesus, I thank you that my inheritance in Christ is not based on my good works but it is based on my faith in Jesus Christ and his finished works. Father I thank you that the inheritance is based on the promise and not on the law, for the law cannot justified me or anybody. Jesus Christ is the justifier of me and anyone who accepted him, in Jesus name, Amen.

¹⁹ Wherefore then serveth the law? It was added because of transgressions, till the seed should come to whom the promise was made; and it was ordained by angels in the hand of a mediator.

Father in the name of Jesus, I thank you that the law did wake my conscious about sins, but the law could not redeem me form sins, Father I thank you for sending Jesus Christ to me, to redeem me from sins. Now I am free from sins, in Jesus name, Amen.

²⁰ Now a mediator is not a mediator of one, but God is one.

Father in the name of Jesus, I thank you for given the new covenant made in the blood of Jesus Christ to Jesus

Christ to be the mediator. I thank you Father that since Jesus Christ is the mediator of the new covenant nobody can deprive me from my inheritance, in Jesus name, Amen.

²¹ Is the law then against the promises of God? God forbid: for if there had been a law given which could have given life, verily righteousness should have been by the law.

Father in the name of Jesus, I thank you that the law is not against the promises, Father I thank you that the law awoken my consciousness about sin, but the promises brought knowledge of deliverer from sins to me, the man Jesus Christ, in Jesus name, Amen.

²² But the scripture hath concluded all under sin, that the promise by faith of Jesus Christ might be given to them that believe.

Father in the name of Jesus, I thank you that all have sin and fall short of your glory, Father I thank you that the wages of sin is death, but your gift to all who have accepted Jesus Christ into their heart is eternal life through Jesus Christ. Father I thank you that I have accepted Jesus Christ in to my heart, I do have eternal life and I do have the promises, in Jesus name, Amen.

²³ But before faith came, we were kept under the law, shut up unto the faith which should afterwards be revealed.

Father in Jesus name, I thank you for your grace, Father I thank you for Jesus Christ, before I accepted Jesus Christ into my heart, I was living by some of the law, my feelings were up sometimes and down sometimes, my desire is to keep the law, but what I will to do, I do not, and what I will not to do, I do, then I accepted Jesus Christ, Jesus Christ set me free, now I am free indeed forever. Thanks be unto God who always gives me the victory through my Lord Jesus Christ, in Jesus name, Amen.

24 Wherefore the law was our schoolmaster to bring us unto Christ, that we might be justified by faith.

Father in the name of Jesus, I thank you that the law did reveal sin to me and also revealed to me that all have sin and come short of the glory of God,

the law reveal to me, he or she that
does not do all the laws is a sinner,
therefore I needed Jesus Christ who
came to fulfill all the law for my sake.
Therefore, now, Jesus Christ, I accepted you into my heart, I am now justified by my faith in Jesus Christ and his
finished works, in Jesus name, Amen.

²⁵ But after that faith is come, we are no longer under a schoolmaster.

Father in the name of Jesus, I thank
you that faith comes by hearing and
hearing by your word. Father I thank
you that Jesus Christ said he is the
Way, the Truth and the Life, Father I
thank you that Jesus Christ is the only
Way to you; therefore I do not need
the law anymore, since Christ in me is
the hope of glory. To you Father I give
all the praises and glory, in Jesus
name, Amen.

²⁶ For ye are all the children of God by faith in Christ Jesus.

Father in the name of Jesus, I thank you that I am your very own Child and you are my very own Father. Father I thank you that the very moment I accepted Jesus Christ into my heart, I became your Child and you became my Father. Now, I belong to you and you belong to me, in Jesus name, Amen.

²⁷ For as many of you as have been baptized into Christ have put on Christ.

Father in Jesus name, I thank you that the moment I accepted Jesus Christ into my heart; I was baptized into the body of Jesus Christ, I became bone of his bone and flesh of is flesh, Father I thank you that this is true of every believer. Father I pray that I will always see believers as the body of Christ here on earth, in Jesus name, Amen.

28 There is neither Jew nor Greek, there is neither bond nor free, there is neither male nor female: for ye are all one in Christ Jesus.

Father in the name of Jesus, I thank you that the moment I accepted Jesus Christ into my heart as my Saviour and Lord, I became part of the body of Jesus Christ. Everybody that has accepted Jesus Christ into his or her heart are part of the body of Jesus Christ, Father I thank you that there is not one person in the body of Christ that is superior to another person in the body of Christ. Father I thank you that there is not one person in the body of Christ that is inferior to another person in the body of Christ. Father in the name of Jesus Christ, I bound every spirit and the spirit behind religion that will make anybody in the body of Christ to feel inferior to anyone else in the body of Christ or to any leadership. Father I thank you that every believer in Jesus Christ are one and member of the body of Jesus Christ. Father I thank you that by your grace I will not see any believer in Jesus Christ superior or inferior, but I see each believer as a brethren, in Jesus name, Amen.

²⁹ And if ye be Christ's, then are ye Abraham's seed, and heirs according to the promise.

Father in the name of Jesus, I thank you that I am in Christ, Father I thank you that I am Abraham's seed, Father I thank you that I am heir according to the promise, Father I thank you that your promise to Abraham's seed belongs to me, in Jesus name, Amen.

CHAPTER FOUR

[1] Now I say, That the heir, as long as he is a child, differeth nothing from a servant, though he be lord of all;

Father in the name of Jesus, I thank you for my birth right, Father I thank you that I will not allow religion, rituals, and the evil one to deprave me of my birth right, in Jesus name, Amen.

[2] But is under tutors and governors until the time appointed of the father.

Father in the name of Jesus, I thank you that you have been with me from my childhood even though I did not know you, but you knew me and destiny me for greatness, a million of thanks to you my very own Father and this is your very own child, in Jesus name, Amen.

³ Even so we, when we were children, were in bondage under the elements of the world:

Father in the name of Jesus, I thank you that when I was a child, I did talk and act as a child, I did sometime follow the dictate of my senses, but as I grow in grace and faith I put away childish way of life, in Jesus name, Amen.

⁴ But when the fulness of the time was come, God sent forth his Son, made of a woman, made under the law,

Father in the name of Jesus, I thank you for sending Jesus Christ in the fullness of time to pay the price for redemption. Jesus Christ I thank you for the great price you paid for my re-demption, Father I thank you that since Jesus Christ paid for my redemption, I must not again pay for my redemption, Jesus paid in full for my redemption, Father I thank you that I do not have to perform any religious rituals for my redemption, Father I thank you that I do not have to earn what I already pos-sess, in Jesus name, Amen.

⁵ To redeem them that were under the law, that we might receive the adoption of sons.

Father in the name of Jesus, I thank you for the great price Jesus Christ paid for my salvation, I accept Jesus Christ scarified for me, now I am a child of God and it do not yet appear how I shall be, but I know that when he shall appear I shall be like him, for I shall see him as he is, Father I thank you that everything begat his or its kind, Father I thank you that according to your word in the book of James, of your own will you begat us(me) with the word of truth, Father I thank you that I am your kind, in Jesus name, Amen.

⁶ And because ye are sons, God hath sent forth the Spirit of his Son into your hearts, crying, Abba, Father.

Father in the name of Jesus, I thank you that I am your child and you have given me your Spirit, Father I thank you that as Jesus is, so I am in this present evil world, in Jesus name, Amen.

⁷ Wherefore thou art no more a servant, but a son; and if a son, then an heir of God through Christ.

Father in the name of Jesus, I thank you that I am no more a servant but your child, your heir and joint-heir with Christ Jesus, now I have rights and privileges, in Jesus name, Amen.

[8] Howbeit then, when ye knew not God, ye did service unto them which by nature are no gods.

Father in the name of Jesus, I thank you for Jesus Christ who you sent to bring salvation to me, Before I accepted Jesus Christ I was hoping that good works is sufficient for righteousness and to please you, but I was completely wrong and empty within, then I accepted Jesus Christ into my heart, all my spiritual search came to an end. All I needed and all I was looking for, I found in Jesus Christ, Father I thank you that Christ is my all in all, in Jesus name, Amen.

⁹ But now, after that ye have known God, or rather are known of God, how turn ye again to the weak and beggarly elements, whereunto ye desire again to be in bondage?

Father in the name of Jesus, I thank you that who the Son set free is free indeed, Father I thank you for salvation and the liberty I have in you, in the name of Jesus Christ of Nazareth, I boldly stand against any entanglement with religion, rituals, worship of any human being or religion denomination. Father in the name of Jesus Christ, my total allegiance is to you and Christ, in Jesus name, Amen.

¹⁰ Ye observe days, and months, and times, and years.

Father in the name of Jesus, I thank you that who the Son set free is free indeed. Father I thank you that I do worship you, Father I thank you that I do not worship Sunday, I do not worship Sabbath, Father I thank you, that you are the True God whom I worship, Father I thank you that I do worship you every day. My allegiance is to God Almighty not to a day or any religious rituals, in Jesus name, Amen.

[11] I am afraid of you, lest I have bestowed upon you labour in vain.

Father in the name of Jesus, I thank you that my labour in the gospel is not in vain, Father I thank you that you have sent me forth in the name of Jesus to proclaim the gospel of my Lord Jesus Christ, you did not sent me forth to proclaim religion or rituals, but to proclaim Jesus Christ and him crucified, died, buried and rose triumphantly. Father in the name of Jesus, I thank you that your word that comes to me is not in vain, for I do mix your word with faith, and your word is profitable to me, in Jesus name, Amen.

¹² Brethren, I beseech you, be as I am; for I am as ye are: ye have not injured me at all.

Father in the name of Jesus, I thank you that your word says follow me as I follow Christ, Father I thank you for your word said I should judge prophesies, Father I thank you for you said you will not have me to be ignorant, Father I thank you for your word said I should watch and pray, Father I thank you for your word said looking unto Jesus who is the Author and Finisher of my faith. Father I thank you that my eyes are on Jesus, Father I thank you for the grace and the joy to read your word daily and to meditate on your word daily, Father I thank you that your word does give me direction in this life and does instruct me about the life to come, in Jesus name, Amen.

¹³ Ye know how through infirmity of the flesh I preached the gospel unto you at the first.

Father in the name of Jesus, I thank you that I am crucified with Christ: nevertheless I live; yet not I, but Christ liveth in me: and the life which I now live in the flesh, I live by the faith of the Son of God, who loved me, and gave himself for me. Therefore, I continue to minister regardless of how I feel, Father I thank you that your word is sufficient for me, in Jesus name, Amen.

¹⁴ And my temptation which was in my flesh ye despised not, nor rejected; but re-

ceived me as an angel of God, even as Christ Jesus.

Father in the name of Jesus, I thank you for your word, Father your word said Christians should receive one another as Christ has received us, Father I thank you that I do fellowship with true believers regardless of what denomination they belongs, in Jesus name I boldly receive other believers as Christ has received me. In the name of Jesus Christ of Nazareth, I bound the spirit of religion and racism that create division in the body of Christ in the Western Hemisphere, in Jesus name, Amen.

[15] Where is then the blessedness ye spake of? for I bear you record, that, if it had been possible, ye would have

plucked out your own eyes, and have given them to me.

Father in the name of Jesus, I thank you that my labour in the gospel is not in vain, Father I thank you that you are not unrighteous to reward me and others that have labored for you in the gospel of our Lord Jesus Christ, Father faithful is you that call me, faithful is you that will reward me in this present world and in the world to come, in Jesus name, Amen.

[16] Am I therefore become your enemy, because I tell you the truth?

Father in the name of Jesus, I thank you that you said in your word that believers should not lie one to another, Father your word said believers should speak the truth in love, Father I thank you for your abounding grace in me to always speak the truth in love, regardless who I am speaking to or who is in my present. Father I pray that I will always please you and not people, in Jesus name, Amen.

¹⁷ They zealously affect you, but not well; yea, they would exclude you, that ye might affect them.

Father in the name of Jesus, I pray that I will not subject myself to any group or organization that profess to be Christian that will use any vice or position to spiritually enslave me, By the grace of God Almighty, I refuse to entangle with any yoke of bondage, in Jesus name, Amen.

¹⁸ But it is good to be zealously affected always in a good thing, and not only when I am present with you.

Father in the name of Jesus, I thank
you for the zeal of the Holy Ghost in
me, Father I thank you that this zeal
will always manifest not only when I
am among fellow believers, but also
when I am among unbelievers. Father I
thank you that your zeal has taken full
control of me, because of your zeal in
me I am not ashamed of the gospel,
because of your zeal in me I have no
problem in acting on your word privately and publicly, in Jesus name,
Amen.

¹⁹ My little children, of whom I travail in birth again until Christ be formed in you,

Father in the name of Jesus, I pray that
I will continue to pray for those I have
shared the gospel of Jesus Christ with,
not to quit praying for them but to continue to trust you that your word which
I have given to them will not return to
you void but it will accomplish that

which you please, and it shall prosper in the thing where to you sent it. Father in the name of Jesus I will continue to see them the ways you see them, I will continue to speak to those things that be not as though they were, in Jesus name, Amen.

²⁰ I desire to be present with you now, and to change my voice; for I stand in doubt of you.

Father in the name of Jesus, I thank you that I did start in the spirit and by your grace I will continue in the spirit, I will not entangle in the law and religious rituals, in Jesus name, Amen.

²¹ Tell me, ye that desire to be under the law, do ye not hear the law?

Father in the name of Jesus, I pray for
the brethren who are still striving to
live by the law, that the eyes of their
understanding will be enlightened; that
they may know what is the hope of
their calling, and what is the riches of
the glory of their inheritance in the
saints, and what is the exceeding
greatness of your power to us ward
who believe, according to the working
of your mighty power, which you
wrought in Christ, when you raised
him from the dead, and set him on
your own right hand in the heavenly
places, far above all principality, and
power, and might, and dominion, and
every name that is named, not only in
this world, but also in that which is
come: I pray they will behold Jesus
Christ and his finished works has they
read your word, in Jesus name, Amen.

22 For it is written, that Abraham had two sons, the

one by a bondmaid, the other by a freewoman.

Father in the name of Jesus, I thank you that the law could not and cannot give life, but Jesus Christ came so that I may have life and have life more abundantly, in Jesus name, Amen.

²³ But he who was of the bondwoman was born after the flesh; but he of the free-woman was by promise.

Father in the name of Jesus, I thank you that the flesh profit nothing, Father I thank you that the new covenant which is of promise, is greater and better than the old covenant which is of the law. Father I thank you for the promise, Father I thank you that I do belong to the promise, in Jesus name, Amen.

24 **Which things are an allegory: for these are the two covenants; the one from the mount Sinai, which gendereth to bondage, which is Agar.**

Father in the name of Jesus, I thank you that you have given me a better covenant establish in the blood of my Lord Jesus Christ, yes better than the law, it is an everlasting covenant, for Christ lives forever, Christ in me the hope of glory, in Jesus name, Amen.

25 **For this Agar is mount Sinai in Arabia, and answereth to Jerusalem which now is, and is in bondage with her children.**

Father in the name of Jesus, I thank you that the new covenant is greater than the old covenant, Father I thank you that the new covenant is sealed with the precious blood of Jesus Christ. I thank you Father that the covenant I do have with you was sealed with the precious blood of Jesus Christ, it is the new covenant, in Jesus name, Amen.

26 But Jerusalem which is above is free, which is the mother of us all.

Father in the name of Jesus, I thank you for who the Son set free is free indeed, I am free indeed, yes free from every yoke of bondage, Father I thank you for the liberty you gave to me in Christ Jesus, Father I thank you that I am daily enjoying the liberty you gave to me in Christ, in Jesus name, Amen.

27 For it is written, Rejoice, thou barren that bearest not;

break forth and cry, thou that travailest not: for the desolate hath many more children than she which hath an husband.

Father in the name of Jesus, I thank you for Jesus Christ, for the laws were many but all the laws was fulfilled in Jesus Christ, Father in Jesus name I thank you that I am not under the law but I am under Christ, in the name of Jesus Christ, I refuse for religion, religious leaders, and the devil to bring me back under the law, henceforth let no man trouble me: for I bear in my body the marks of the Lord Jesus, I do have the mind of Christ, in Christ I live, move and have my being, in Jesus name, Amen.

28 Now we, brethren, as Isaac was, are the children of promise.

Father in the name of Jesus, I thank you that as Isaac was a child of promise, so am I; I am also a child of promise. Father I thank you for Jesus Christ who through his death brought me into the promise, in Jesus name, Amen.

29 But as then he that was born after the flesh persecuted him that was born after the Spirit, even so it is now.

Father in the name of Jesus, I thank you that you always cause me to triumphant in Christ Jesus, Father I thank you that you said the flesh always strife against the spirit, Father I thank you that I am in the Spirit and I do walk in the Spirit, and I do not fulfill the lust of the flesh, I am led daily by the Spirit, not by my flesh or senses, Father I thank you that I am spiritually minded, in Jesus name, Amen.

³⁰ Nevertheless what saith the scripture? Cast out the bondwoman and her son: for the son of the bondwoman shall not be heir with the son of the freewoman.

Father in the name of Jesus, I thank you that because Jesus Christ paid the ultimate and vicarious price to redeem me, I do not live by the law and Jesus, I solemnly live for Jesus Christ who love me and gave himself for me. Jesus Christ is God manifested in the flesh. God is love, I do live in God's love, whatever I do in word or deed, I do it in love, I have no fear because perfect love cast out fear, God's love in me is perfect, in Jesus name, Amen.

³¹ So then, brethren, we are not children of the bond-woman, but of the free.

Father in the name of Jesus, I thank you that I am no longer under the law, Father I thank you that Jesus Christ fulfilled the law for me, by his death on the cross. I am crucified with Christ: nevertheless I live; yet not I, but Christ liveth in me: and the life which I now live in the flesh I live by the faith of the Son of God, who loved me, and gave himself for me. Father I thank you that who the Son set free, is free indeed. Father I thank you that I do not go around establishing my own righteousness. Father I thank you for you have made Christ Jesus unto me wisdom, and righteousness, and sanctification, and redemption, in Jesus name, Amen.

CHAPTER FIVE

[1] Stand fast therefore in the liberty wherewith Christ hath made us free, and be not entangled again with the yoke of bondage.

Father in the name of Jesus, I thank you for Jesus Christ; I thank you for the redemption Jesus Christ purchased for me. Father I thank you for the liberty Jesus Christ purchased and gave to me, I am free, forever free, never to entangled with religious yoke. I refuse to be bound; I refuse to entangle again with the yoke of bondage, in Jesus name, Amen.

[2] Behold, I Paul say unto you, that if ye be circumcised,

Christ shall profit you nothing.

Father in the name of Jesus, I thank you that Jesus Christ came to fulfill the law for me, since all the laws are fulfilled in Jesus Christ, I am no longer require to live by the laws, if there is any law I should live by, it is faith in the law of the new kind of love Jesus Christ brought to the world for the new race of people he purchased with his own precious blood, I do live in the law of God's commandment of love, in Jesus name, Amen.

³ For I testify again to every man that is circumcised, that he is a debtor to do the whole law.

Father in the name of Jesus, I thank you for sending Jesus Christ to me, for you know me and I know me, that I cannot live by the whole law, so Father I am very grateful to you for Jesus Christ fulfillment of the law for me, I now go forth to live for Christ who loved me and gave himself for me, in Jesus name, Amen.

⁴ Christ is become of no effect unto you, whosoever of you are justified by the law; ye are fallen from grace.

Father in the name of Jesus, I thank you that I am justified by faith in Jesus Christ and his finished works, because I accepted Jesus Christ as my Saviour and Lord, I am a new creature in Christ, old things are pass away, and behold all things are become new, in Jesus name, Amen.

⁵ For we through the Spirit wait for the hope of right-eousness by faith.

Father in the name of Jesus, I thank you that I through the Spirit do wait for the hope of righteousness by faith, Father I thank you that Jesus Christ is my righteousness, for you have made Jesus Christ unto me righteousness, in Jesus name, Amen.

⁶ For in Jesus Christ neither circumcision availeth any thing, nor uncircumcision; but faith which worketh by love.

Father in the name of Jesus, I thank you that in Jesus Christ all believers are one, none is superior to others and none is inferior to others. Father I thank you that no believer is above another believer, and no believer is below another believer, Father I thank you that every believer are saved by grace through faith in Jesus Christ, Father I thank you that there is no salvation in any other, Father I thank you that salvation is only in the name of Jesus Christ, in Jesus name, amen.

^{7} Ye did run well; who did hinder you that ye should not obey the truth?

Father in the name of Jesus, I thank you that I am obedient to the truth, I started by faith through grace and I do continue to live for you by faith through grace. Father by your grace I will not turn from the truth and go to religion. Father I thank you that through your grace I do read your word daily and I do talk to you daily. Father I thank you that you do talk to me daily through your word, prayer, your Holy Spirit that dwells in me, and by any other means you choose that is not contrary to your word. Father I thank you that through your grace I do not look for or search for some deep revelation, Father I thank you that your written word is sufficient and more than enough for me, in Jesus name, Amen.

⁸ This persuasion cometh not of him that calleth you.

Father in the name of Jesus, I thank you that you are not the author of confusion, but of peace. Father I thank you that you do not contradict your word, Father in the name of Jesus, I thank you that you do speak peace to your people, in Jesus name, Amen.

⁹ A little leaven leaveneth the whole lump.

Father in the name of Jesus, I thank you that by your grace I will not allow sin into my life, I will fight the good fight of faith, I will hold on to eternal life, I will judge myself, so that I will not be judge, your grace is sufficient, greater is he that is me than he that is in the world, Father whenever I miss the mark I will run to you and not from you, for you are my very own Father and I am your very own child, in Jesus name, Amen.

¹⁰ I have confidence in you through the Lord, that ye will be none otherwise minded: but he that troubleth you shall bear his judgment, whosoever he be.

Father in the name of Jesus, I thank you that my duty in life is to serve you, Father I thank you that you said I should be careful for nothing, Father you never want me to worry no matter what the circumstances may be, because you are my very own Father and I am your very own child, and you do faithfully take care of me, you told me to cast all my cares upon you for you care for me, Father in Jesus name I do

consciously and deliberately cast all
my cares upon you, for you do care for
me, in Jesus name, Amen.

¹¹ And I, brethren, if I yet preach circumcision, why do I yet suffer persecution? then is the offence of the cross ceased.

Father in Jesus name, I thank you that
you called me to follow you, Father I
thank you that Jesus Christ died for
me, Father I thank you that religion did
not died for me, therefore, I will not
follow religion and ritual, Father I
thank you that I am crucified unto the
world and the world is crucified unto
me. Father I thank you that I do talk
about Jesus Christ and not about religion, Father I thank you that I preach
Jesus Christ and not religion, Father I
thank you that my heart desire is to

always please you not to please people,
in Jesus name, Amen.

¹² I would they were even cut off which trouble you.

Father in the name of Jesus, I thank
you that you said vengeance is yours,
yes, Father I thank you that vengeance
is not mine, so I will continue to serve
you, worship you and sing unto you
while you fight my battle, in Jesus
name, Amen.

¹³ For, brethren, ye have been called unto liberty; only use not liberty for an occasion to the flesh, but by love serve one another.

Father in the name of Jesus, I thank
you for the liberty Jesus Christ gave to
me, Father I thank you that I am enjoying my liberty in Christ Jesus regard-

less what religious folks think or may say about me, for who the Son sets free is free indeed, Father I thank you that I am free indeed, with my liberty in Christ I do walk in love, and I do love me and others as Christ loves me, in Jesus name, Amen.

¹⁴ For all the law is fulfilled in one word, even in this; Thou shalt love thy neighbour as thyself.

Father in Jesus name, I thank you that Jesus Christ fulfilled the whole law, Father I thank you that you are Love, Father I thank you that Jesus Christ proceeded from you, and I did proceeded from Jesus Christ, Father you said you begat me by your word. Father you gave birth to me by your word, Father I thank you that Jesus Christ is your word, Father I thank you that I did proceed out of Love, Father I thank you that you are a Lover, so I am, I am a lover, Father I thank you that I do love my neighbour as myself. Father I thank you that the measure I love myself, is the measure I will love my neighbour, I cannot love my neighbour more or less than I love myself, Father I thank you for your grace in my life for me to love myself regardless what anyone think or say about me, Father I thank you that what matter is what you think of me, for I am fully persuaded that you think good of me continuously, and I do think good of me always. in Jesus name, Amen.

¹⁵ But if ye bite and devour one another, take heed that ye be not consumed one of another.

Father in the name of Jesus, I thank you that you are not the author of confusion, Father I thank you that you are the God of peace, Father I thank you that I am a child of peace, Father I thank you that I do follow peace with everyone, Father I thank you that I do pursue peace daily, in Jesus name, Amen.

¹⁶ This I say then, Walk in the Spirit, and ye shall not fulfil the lust of the flesh.

Father in the name of Jesus, I thank you that I am in Christ, Father I thank you that I do live by your word, Father I thank you that I do walk in the Spirit and I do not fulfill the lust of the flesh, in Jesus name, Amen.

¹⁷ For the flesh lusteth against the Spirit, and the Spirit against the flesh: and these are contrary the one to

the other: so that ye cannot do the things that ye would.

Father in the name of Jesus, I thank you that I am redeemed, Father I thank you that I do buffet my flesh, Father I thank you that I do use your word to put my flesh in subjection to your will for me, yes, when my flesh do not want me to pray by telling me that I am tired, I refuse the flesh excuse, and I take stance to pray, Father I thank you for my prayer life, in Jesus name, Amen.

[18] But if ye be led of the Spirit, ye are not under the law.

Father in the name of Jesus, I thank you that I am led by the Spirit and I am not under the law. Father I thank you that Jesus Christ has fulfill the law for me, Father I thank you that what Jesus Christ carried and paid for in my stead, I need not and I will not carry or pay for it again, regardless of theologians teachings and religious teachings, in Jesus name, I am forever free from the law, in Jesus name I boldly refuse to be bring back under the law, I do fight the good fight of faith, Christ is all in all, in Jesus name, Amen.

[19] Now the works of the flesh are manifest, which are these; Adultery, fornication, uncleanness, lasciviousness,

Father in the name of Jesus, I thank you that I do walk in the Spirit, and I do not fulfill the lust of the flesh. Father I thank you that I am led by your Spirit, Father I thank you that I do bring my flesh under the leadership of the Spirit, Father I thank you that I do buffet my flesh, Father I thank you that as I pray in the spirit and in all kinds of prayers and as I act on your word daily I do bring my flesh and feelings under the subjection of the Holy Spirit, in Jesus name, Amen.

20 Idolatry, witchcraft, hatred, variance, emulations, wrath, strife, seditions, heresies,

Father in the name of Jesus, I thank you that Jesus Christ has set me free, who the Son sets free is free indeed, I am free indeed, Father I thank you that your word said I am not in the flesh but in the Spirit, I boldly say I am not in the flesh, but I am in the Spirit, in Jesus name, Amen.

21 Envyings, murders, drunkenness, revellings, and such like: of the which I tell you before, as I have also told you in time past, that they which do such things shall

not inherit the kingdom of God.

Father in the name of Jesus, I thank you for Jesus Christ who delivered me from darkness and translated me into his marvelous light. Father I thank you that I am born again, Father I thank you that I am a new creature, Father I thank you that you are my Father and I am your child, in Jesus name, Amen.

²² But the fruit of the Spirit is love, joy, peace, longsuffering, gentleness, goodness, faith,

Father in the name of Jesus, I thank you that the fruit of the Spirit is your manifestation in the human arena, Father in the name of Jesus I thank you for the manifestation of yourself through me by the fruit of the Spirit that is seen and acknowledge by eve-

ryone that I come in contact with, in
Jesus name, Amen.

²³ Meekness, temperance: against such there is no law.

Father in the name of Jesus, I thank
you that I do live in your love, Father I
thank you that I do walk in your love,
Father I thank you that you are a Lover, and whatever is true of you is true
of me, Father I thank you that I am a
lover, Father I thank you that Jesus
Christ fulfilled the law, Father I thank
you that there is no law against love, in
Jesus name, Amen.

²⁴ And they that are Christ's have crucified the flesh with the affections and lusts.

Father in the name of Jesus, I thank
you that I am crucified unto the world
and the world is crucified unto me, I
no longer have appetite for the world,

for all that is in the world, is the lust of the flesh, and the lust of the eyes, and the pride of life. Father I thank you that I am in the world but not of the world, Father I thank you that I am your ambassador in Christ, Father I thank you that Jesus Christ has sent me into the world, just as you sent him into the world, therefore, I go forth into the world in the name of Jesus with all the authority that is in the name of Jesus, in Jesus name, Amen.

25 If we live in the Spirit, let us also walk in the Spirit.

Father in the name of Jesus, I thank you that I do live in the Spirit and I do walk in the Spirit, my fellowship with you is unbreakable, Father I thank you that I am a doer of your word, in Jesus name, Amen.

26 Let us not be desirous of vain glory, provoking one

another, envying one another.

Father in the name of Jesus, I thank you that I am crucified unto the world and the world is crucified unto me. Father I thank you that I do not seek for the honour that comes from man, people or the populous, I only seek the honour that comes from you. Father I thank you that I am delivered from people, Father I thank you that what matter is what you think of me and what your word says about me. Father I thank you that you do always think good of me. Father I thank you that your word does say good and great things about me. Father I thank you that I am who your word said that I am, I have what your word said Jesus Christ died and purchase for me, and I can do what your word says I can do. Father I thank you that there is no limit to the good that I can do, for I can do

all things through Christ who strength-
en me, in Jesus name, Amen.

CHAPTER SIX

¹ Brethren, if a man be over-taken in a fault, ye which are spiritual, restore such an one in the spirit of meekness; considering thyself, lest thou also be tempted.

Father in the name of Jesus, I thank you that I am standing by your grace not in my strength, I thank you for the grace to reach out to any fallen brethren, to minister your love and grace to them, in Jesus name, Amen.

² Bear ye one another's burdens, and so fulfil the law of Christ.

Father in the name of Jesus, I thank you that your word said by this shall everyone know that I am your disciple, if I love other believers in Christ. Father I thank you that I am my brothers and sisters keeper, Father I thank you for the grace to always intercede for other believers, in Jesus name, Amen.

[3] For if a man think himself to be something, when he is nothing, he deceiveth himself.

Father in the name of Jesus, I ask for the grace to never think of myself above any believer no matter what the circumstance may be, also never to think of myself below any minister or Preacher. Father I thank you for your word said they measuring themselves by themselves, and comparing themselves among themselves, are not wise, Father I thank you that I do have the mind of Christ and Jesus Christ is made unto me wisdom, Father I thank you that I am wise, in Jesus name, Amen.

⁴ But let every man prove his own work, and then shall he have rejoicing in himself alone, and not in another.

Father in Jesus name, I thank you for your word said I should make my moderation be known to all people, for the Lord is at hand, Father I thank you that your word said whatever I do in word or deed, I should do it to the glory of God in Christ Jesus. Father I thank you that Jesus Christ only seek the honour that comes from you, not the honour that comes from people. Father by your grace I set my whole heart to only seek the honour that comes from you alone. I do not seek the honour that comes from people, in Jesus name, Amen.

5 For every man shall bear his own burden.

Father in the name of Jesus, I thank you that your grace is sufficient for me in every situation, Father I thank you that through your grace I can surely stand on your unfailing word, in Jesus name, Amen.

6 Let him that is taught in the word communicate unto him that teacheth in all good things.

Father in the name of Jesus, I thank you for your word said the labourer is worthy of his hirer, Father I thank you that your word is truth, Father I thank you that you are able to make all grace abound toward me that I will always have everything in sufficiency, that I may abound unto every good works. Father I thank you that you do reward anyone that give in the right way, Father I thank you that I am a giver and I am a receiver, in Jesus name, Amen.

[7] Be not deceived; God is not mocked: for whatsoever a man soweth, that shall he also reap.

Father in the name of Jesus, your word said as the earth remaineth there will be seedtime and harvest, Father I judge you faithful, as Sarah judge you faithful that has promise. Father I thank you that you do reward faithfulness, Father ask for your grace for me to stay faithful to you no matter the circumstances, for the suffering of this present time is not worthy to be compare to the glory which shall be reveal in me and through me, in Jesus name, Amen.

⁸ For he that soweth to his flesh shall of the flesh reap corruption; but he that soweth to the Spirit shall of the Spirit reap life everlasting.

Father in the name of Jesus, I thank you for your law of sowing and reaping. Father I thank you that you spoke the law into existence for my benefit. Father I thank you that by your grace I do sow to the Spirit, I do read your word, I do mediate in your word, I do act on your word, and I do sow good and great seed. Father I thank you for my harvest. Father I thank you for making all grace abound toward me, that I will ways have all sufficiency in all things, may abound to every good work: in Jesus name, Amen.

⁹ And let us not be weary in well doing: for in due season we shall reap, if we faint not.

Father in the name of Jesus, I thank you that your grace will always stand tall in every situation, so that Jesus Christ may be glorify. Father I thank you that your grace is sufficient for me in every circumstance I face, therefore by your grace I am not weary in well doing, in Jesus name, Amen.

¹⁰ As we have therefore opportunity, let us do good unto all men, especially unto them who are of the household of faith.

Father in the name of Jesus, I pray that I will not ignore a brother or a sister in need, when I can reach out to help them, for all I have and all I will ever possess is from you, Father I pray that

I will be a good steward of all you have put in my possession, in Jesus name, Amen.

11 Ye see how large a letter I have written unto you with mine own hand.

Father in the name of Jesus, I thank you that by your grace I will keep communication and fellowship with fellow believers, Father I thank you that I am an agent of encouragement, in Jesus name, Amen.

12 As many as desire to make a fair shew in the flesh, they constrain you to be circumcised; only lest they should suffer persecution for the cross of Christ.

Father in the name of Jesus, I thank you for the relationship you and I have together, Father I thank you that I do not have to proof anything to anybody about our relationship. Father I thank you for your grace in my life for me not to compromise my relationship with you, Father I thank you for the grace not to allow religion and ritual into my life, in Jesus name, Amen.

13 For neither they themselves who are circumcised keep the law; but desire to have you circumcised, that they may glory in your flesh.

Father in the name of Jesus, I thank you that by your grace I will not accept religion into life, I do boldly refuse to please any religious person, Christ is all in all, in Jesus name, Amen.

14 But God forbid that I should glory, save in the cross of our Lord Jesus

Christ, by whom the world is crucified unto me, and I unto the world.

Father in the name of Jesus, I thank you that I do glory in you, Father I thank you that in you alone do I glory, I am crucified unto the world and the world is crucified unto me, in Jesus name, Amen.

¹⁵ For in Christ Jesus neither circumcision availeth any thing, nor uncircumcision, but a new creature.

Father in the name of Jesus, I thank you that I am part of the body of Christ, Father I thank you that in the body of Christ, all born again are one. Father I thank you that no person in the body of Christ is more important than another person in the body of Christ, Father I thank you that Christ is the head of this body, in Jesus name, Amen.

¹⁶ And as many as walk according to this rule, peace be on them, and mercy, and upon the Israel of God.

Father in the name of Jesus, I thank you and I pray for those brethren in the body of Christ that are sowing division in the body of Christ, that you will forgive them and that you will open their eyes to behold Jesus Christ and his suffering on the cross. Father in the name of Jesus Christ by your grace I am committed to sow peace in the body of Christ, in Jesus name, Amen.

¹⁷ From henceforth let no man trouble me: for I bear in my body the marks of the Lord Jesus.

Father in the name of Jesus, I thank you that your grace do abound in me, Father I thank you that Christ in me is the hope of glory, Father I thank you that you that is in me is greater than he that is in the world, I quit me like man, having done all I stand, I will not allow religion into life, in Jesus name, Amen.

[18] Brethren, the grace of our Lord Jesus Christ be with your spirit. Amen.

Father in the name of Jesus, I do receive your grace and I immense my spirit, soul, and body into your manifold grace, in Jesus name, Amen.

SOIL Foundation, Inc.

All Books can be Purchase from amazon.com, Amazon.co.uk, Amazon.de, Amazon.fr, Amazon.it, Amazon.es, Barnesandnoble.com, ebay.com, createspace.com (search: Ovbije Book)

Publication Books

All Day God

Praying the Word From the Book of Timothy

Praying the Word From the Book of Ephesians

Resurrection from the Flood

Coaching to Completion

Praying the Word From the Epistle of John

God Loves Me

God Is With Me I Am Not Afraid

Praying the Word From the Book of Galatians

<u>Tracts:</u>

5 Things God wants you to know

Love Yourself

THE TEN COMMANDMENTS

1. You shall have no other gods before me.

2. You shall not make idols.

3. You shall not take the name of the LORD your God in vain.

4. Remember the Sabbath day, to keep it holy.

5. Honor your father and your mother.

6. You shall not murder.

7. You shall not commit adultery.

8. You shall not steal.

9. You shall not bear false witness against your neighbor.

10. You shall not covet.

Jesus said "A new commandment I give unto you, That ye love one another; as I have loved you, that ye also love one another." St. John 13:34

SONG

<u>JESUS WILL NEVER TURN YOU DOWN</u>

Jesus is a friend that will never turn you down

He will never leave you nor forsake you

Call on his name for he is there for you

He will save and guide you to end

He will save and guide you

REPEAT

By L. O. Ovbije

HYMN

Grace Greater Than Our Sin

1. Marvelous grace of our loving Lord,
grace that exceeds our sin and our guilt!
Yonder on Calvary's mount outpoured,
there where the blood of the Lamb was spilt.
Refrain:
Grace, grace, God's grace,
grace that will pardon and cleanse within;
grace, grace, God's grace,
grace that is greater than all our sin!

2. Sin and despair, like the sea waves cold,
threaten the soul with infinite loss;
grace that is greater, yes, grace untold,
points to the refuge, the mighty cross.
(Refrain)

3. Dark is the stain that we cannot hide.
What can avail to wash it away?
Look! There is flowing a crimson tide,
brighter than snow you may be today.
(Refrain)

4. Marvelous, infinite, matchless grace,
freely bestowed on all who believe!
You that are longing to see his face,
will you this moment his grace receive?
(Refrain)

By *Julia H. Johnston*

116

www.ingramcontent.com/pod-product-compliance
Lightning Source LLC
Chambersburg PA
CBHW060527030426
42337CB00015B/2006